A Month of Mondays